LADY OF

POWER

TIFFANY KELLY

The Mind, Body & Power Coach

LADY OF POWER

31 Mind, Body & Power Inspirations for Your
Weight-Loss Journey!

**TRM
Publications**

a division of TRM Enterprises, LLC

Copyright © 2015 Tiffany Kelly
Published by TRM Publications
Post Office Box 16124
Atlanta, Georgia 30321
www.trm-enterprises.com

TRM Publications is a division of
TRM Enterprises, LLC, Atlanta, Georgia

Printed in the United States of America

ISBN 978-0692572146

Cover designed by Gifted Dezyns Graphics Firm, LLC

DEDICATION

First and foremost, I dedicate my first written work to my Lord and Savior Jesus Christ, who has called me to help women live a healthy life. To my mom, Barbara Williams, and my dad, Fred Wright, who always believe I can do anything; my family and friends who never give up on me, and my mentor, Wanda Harmon (deceased), who taught me to always let my work speak for me.

And especially, to all of the women who desire to WIN by ending the dieting cycle and achieving permanent weight-loss success! The POWER is in you!

CONTENTS

INTRODUCTION

The road to weight-loss success is not an easy one shot deal! But as the scripture says, "I can do all things through Christ who strengthens me." (Philippians 4:13, NKJV) If this journey were easy, then everyone would be their ideal weight. There wouldn't be a motivational or inspirational story to tell. God uses us to draw others near to Him by our testimonies. Your story and my story serve as testimonies of God's work, His ability to deliver us, and empower us – in a nutshell, do what man may see as impossible!

This book, *Lady of Power* - and yes, you are a Lady of Power - is for you. You're a woman of God, even when you think you're not. You were created to be a woman of strength. This book was written with you in mind. These 31 Mind, Body & Power Inspirations were created with God's guidance to inspire you to stay encouraged and powered up on your journey to a healthier you! *Lady of Power* is a daily journey through scriptures, words of inspiration and motivation, as well as affirmations to bring God closer to your heart in order to help you rise above the challenges you will have along the weight-loss journey. God has a plan for your life and this book is intended to help you create an atmosphere of faith, positivity, hope, perseverance, and empowerment so that you can stay committed to your journey.

When I wrote each inspiration, I thought about all of my experiences on my weight-loss journey and asked God to give me the words to put on paper that were in season for a time such as this. I wanted to inspire and motivate you every day so that you not only reach your goals and end the dieting cycle, but also to lean more on God and achieve your life's purpose!

Following this introduction, you will find a manifesto I wrote before this book idea existed. The manifesto is titled, "I AM DETERMINATION!" I wrote this manifesto to give every reader a brief synopsis of my journey to weight-loss success and to remind myself of how far God has brought me. When I wrote each inspiration for this book, I reflected upon the challenges I faced and that you, Lady of Power, may face on this journey to weight-loss success. Additionally, I wrote inspirations that reflect challenges I've faced after I reached my weight-loss goal. Along this journey, I have endured many setbacks, but I stay determined to never be defeated because I know that despite what I may see or feel at the moment, it's all in God's plan for my life and for His glory to be manifested.

It's my prayer that after reading my manifesto and your daily Mind, Body & Power Inspirations, you will be deeply motivated and inspired to let God guide you in a mighty way to create a healthier, more powerful and new YOU. May God bless you each and every day along the journey. May each scripture selected touch your heart and serve as a reminder of how God can provide the strength we need each and every day. It is my sincerest hope that every day you open this book, there's a word that is exactly what you needed to read to get you through your day.

Take time to read, reflect, and journal about your journey. Enjoy each day as you build strength, confidence, faith, courage, and compassion. Feel free to go back and reread inspirations that deeply minister to your heart. After reading all thirty-one for the month, it's okay to start over or read them in whatever order suits your journey. Remember, this journey was created by God, especially for you! He has your best interest at heart and is waiting to reward you for making a decision to become healthier so that He can use you for what He created you for! So Lady of Power, it's time to get started. You are more than equipped for this. The POWER is in you!

Manifesto

A Lil' Inspiration…

So when you think you've been defeated, I want you to reflect on all of your victories and know that your best is yet to come! Amen!

I AM DETERMINATION!

When I reflect on my journey to a better me, I can't help but to declare...

I AM DETERMINATION!

You are looking at someone who is a work in progress, destined for greatness and purposed by God...

I AM DETERMINATION!

You are looking at someone who spent twelve years suffering from high blood pressure and is now two years medicine free...

I AM DETERMINATION!

You are looking at someone who lived six years on medication to treat panic attacks and with God's help, took authority, released herself and made a full recovery...

I AM DETERMINATION!

You are looking at someone who was told she didn't have the credentials to become a teacher but became not just a teacher but a Teacher of the Year...

I AM DETERMINATION!

You are looking at someone who has had countless disappointments in relationships with men but refuses to give up because God has someone looking for his Queen...

I AM DETERMINATION!

You are looking at someone who, for most of her early life was a plus-sized woman weighing as much as 262 lbs., has lost over 80 lbs. and works every day to maintain it...

I AM DETERMINATION!

You are looking at someone who has struggled with food and being an emotional eater, and now has control and makes better choices...

I AM DETERMINATION!

You are looking at someone who has battled with depression for the past three years and continues to push through because defeat is not an option...

I AM DETERMINATION!

You are looking at someone whom God has called to

help inspire, empower, and transform lives so that you can take authority and rise above the challenges you face and live a life of unprecedented success...**YOU TOO ARE DETERMINATION!**

BEFORE   **AFTER**

Day *1*
Ask Yourself Why?

》———➤•◀———《

Often, we look for quick fixes to life's challenges. For instance, if we reflect on previous attempts at losing weight, most of us can cite at least three different programs or fad diets we've tried. We look for the quickest way to lose weight because we live in a "microwave" society that wants everything quick. We must recognize that everything has a process for success! This success process is a mindset shift. The reason the quick fix diets didn't result in permanent and lasting change is because your mindset didn't change. Your mind is the key!!

Have you ever reflected on the real reasons you have challenges staying committed to a healthy diet, exercise regimen, or anything else in your life that requires your total commitment? As you begin your weight-loss journey, whether this is your first time or third time, start with a new mindset that you're ready to WIN and make this a permanent change! Take a moment to reflect and ask yourself, "WHY? Why am I unable to resist foods that aren't the best choices? Why am I unable to commit myself to at least three days of exercise a week? Why do I continue to start and stop my journey to good health?" After reflecting on the questions that apply to you, ask yourself, "What steps am I totally committed to taking to make this new journey the start of a permanent lifestyle change?"

This journey is all about you! Are you ready to WIN by breaking the dieting cycle? Do you want to see your life change for good? You are reading this book right now because you're tired of the dieting cycle. You want lasting results. Your desire is to stand poised and strong like never before. Use these powerful inspirations to jump-start or recharge your weight-loss journey. Remember the scripture Philippians 4:13 which says, "I can do all things through Christ who strengthens me." You can do this. Results are coming with the strength of the Holy Spirit! It is my prayer that you will be inspired, motivated, and pushed through these powerful thought-provoking Mind and Body Power Inspirations to stand powerful like never before and reach permanent weight-loss success!! Use these inspirations to uplift yourself and support your weight-loss and life journey. Use the journal pages after each inspiration to reflect on your daily walk during the journey. Share how these inspirations inspire you to push through and WIN daily! Now it's time to WIN and become a more powerful YOU!!

Are you ready? Repeat after me… "I am ready to begin my journey to permanent weight-loss success! I can do this!! I am a WINNER!!"

Wooohooooo!!!!! It's time to WIN, Lady of Power. Let's get this journey started!!!

Your Thoughts:

Day *2*
Take Action! Make Bold Steps! Be Prepared!

$$\gg\!\!\!\longrightarrow\cdot\longleftarrow\!\!\!\ll$$

So you said you're ready to end the dieting cycle, right? How bad do you want it? Do you want it bad enough to give up that favorite fast food restaurant that you frequent? Bad enough that you're willing to carry your meals for lunch and opt out of the daily lunch run with co-workers? Do you want it bad enough to not let your hair be the reason you won't sign up for that fitness class? Yes, I went there! Lol. This journey is not for the faint at heart! It is for you, Lady of Power! It is time to commit to a lifestyle makeover!

This makeover, this new weight-loss journey, requires you to dig deep within to loose the power which God has given you to take action, make bold steps, and be prepared! In the bible, James 2:24 reads, "You see that a person is considered righteous by what they do and not by faith alone." (NIV) Being prepared means putting your beliefs of what you say that you're capable of doing into actions. You may be wondering, what does that mean? It means, winning on this journey to weight-loss success will require eating out less (especially when you first start your journey); making better choices when you do eat out; creating a weekly schedule for working out and/or getting a personal trainer; signing up with a mind, body, and power coach (hint, hint); and finally – but not the least – consistently planning and preparing healthy meals that help you reach your goals.

Do you have people around you who would want you to fail? Do they expect you to repeat the dieting cycle? Do they say things like, "Yeah, she's said that before. Let's see how long she'll last this time. She'll never lose that weight"? Now is the time to shut down your naysayers!! Or as some people call them, "haters!" Make your actions bold! Bold enough for people to take a second look at what you're accomplishing. Take the bold steps of signing up at a local gym, joining a fitness group, or starting one yourself! Be bold and sign-up with a trainer, coach, or dietician, or research on-line for resources that support meal planning and exercise tips.

A part of being bold on this journey means that you'll have to prepare your meals for the week. This is the key to successful weight-loss. Planning your meals and carrying them with you every day will lower your chances of selecting foods that won't help you reach your weight-loss goals! Select a day you'll commit to shopping and cooking your meals for the week. Boldly create a weekly schedule to make fitness a part of your life. Dedicate yourself and be determined to stick to your regimen. Remember, you are no longer on a diet. You are creating a healthy lifestyle makeover for permanent weight-loss success. The cycle is no longer an option!!

Be inspired and motivated to transform your mindset and take bold actions that no longer mirror a powerless woman! Say this to yourself, "I am a Lady of Power who is capable of reaching my weight-loss goals! I will take action by making bold steps because I am prepared!"

Your Thoughts:

_____

_____

_____

_____

_____

_____

_____

_____

_____

_____

_____

_____

_____

_____

_____

_____

_____

_____

_____

_____

Day *3*
What Are You Waiting For?

How many times have you said, "I'm going to start next week. I'll start when I find a new gym. Oh, I'm going to start after I finish the food in my house. I have to do something with my hair before I start at the gym"? Sound familiar? We can go on and on with excuses. These are excuses because they continue to keep you on the vicious cycle and not accomplishing your weight-loss goals! When are you going to step up to the plate, step out in faith, and let God direct your journey to achieving better health? What are you waiting for?

Sometimes before we decide to step out in faith and do what God is calling us to do, we wait for everything to be in perfect order. That's not always the case! All of your questions won't be answered and everything won't be in order before you step out and start your journey. It's only when you trust that God will order your steps, and step out and begin your weight-loss journey that success will happen! The bible says, "Seek his will in all you do, and he will show you which path to take." (Proverbs 3:6, NLT) Therefore, if you trust in him along this journey, God will give you guidance and be there for you every step of the way! Just begin!

If you're waiting for a special feeling, person, thing, or miracle, it may never come. You have to come to the realization that you can't wait another year, month, day, minute, or second to start your journey to better health and a better you! It's never a perfect time – you make the time perfect! Get going and watch your journey take flight! Put your goals for better health as a priority! Envision your goals manifesting in your life and let that fuel your daily determination, dedication, and commitment to your journey to permanent weight-loss success!

It is time to win by getting up and getting started on your weight-loss journey! It's not too late! Tell yourself, "I have everything I need to get started! Everything I need is in me! I will trust that God will give me all I need to stay the course and see my goals for better health manifest! I can do this!"

Your Thoughts:

Day 4
YOU ARE GOD'S GREATEST CREATION!

$$\gg\!\!\!\longrightarrow\cdot\longleftarrow\!\!\!\ll$$

Do you know that you're God's greatest creation? Ephesians 2:10 says, "For we are God's masterpiece. He has created us anew in Christ Jesus, so we can do the good things he has planned for us long ago." (NLT) God had plans for us before we were born (Jeremiah 1:5). Therefore, He knows our needs and intercedes on our behalf. At times, things don't go according to plan. It's easy to get depressed and give up. Today is the day you change your mindset. Tell yourself this, "Everything is working out in my best interest!" Do you know that God will remove you from situations so that He can protect you? When He removes you, He wants to reach you so that you can accomplish what He has purposed for you. Yes! Keep pushing forward because it's in these challenges and disappointments that God is strengthening you for your greatness. The breakthrough is near. Don't miss your turn-around.

Along your weight-loss journey, there'll be times that you will become discouraged because the weight isn't coming off fast enough, finances aren't turning around, or a relationship is on a rocky road. Be encouraged. Your breakthrough moment is here! You are a fighter, strong in faith, and determined to win. The power that has been given to you, no one can take away. Therefore, fight like a soldier to the end. Don't throw in the towel too soon and miss your breakthrough. Continue to be dedicated to your weight-loss journey and have faith that God is your support and He will see you through those tough times. Watch Him give you the strength to stay on track daily. He's got you! Stay the course and get your breakthrough.

Get ready to stand in your power and live the life that has been planned for you, Lady of Power. Tell yourself, "I get better each and every day, I am stronger than I think! I am walking in my power to achieve permanent weight-loss success!"

Your Thoughts:

_____
_____
_____
_____
_____
_____
_____
_____
_____
_____
_____
_____
_____
_____
_____
_____
_____
_____
_____
_____
_____

Day 5
All Things Work For Your Good!

Have you ever asked yourself why every time you start your journey, it seems like major challenges come your way that kick your journey off kilter? Romans 8:28 says, "And we know that in all things God works for the good of those who love him, who have been called according to his purpose." (NIV). Therefore, no matter what your situation looks like, you must know that God is working it out for your good! When you're faced with challenges along your weight-loss journey, take a moment and ask yourself, "Why am I experiencing this? What can I learn from this setback? How can I strategize to be successful on this journey if this happens again? How can I use this experience to help someone else?" Powerful questions, right? You have to believe that God makes no mistakes and that these challenges only build your muscles for permanent success!

Speak positively over everything. Continue to loose your power by daily telling yourself how strong you are and that you'll reach your weight-loss goals! Your extra sexy shape is on its way, along with that dress you've envisioned stepping out in!

Watch how God will set you up to win as He prepares you for an amazing transformation. It's time to uncover the strength that is already in you. Yes you, Lady of Power! Every time challenges come, just smile and say, "I'm going to be extra sexy when He's done with my process because I'm getting stronger with every challenge!"

Your Thoughts:

_____
_____
_____
_____
_____
_____
_____
_____
_____
_____
_____
_____
_____
_____
_____
_____
_____
_____
_____
_____
_____
_____

Day *6*
This Journey Is Custom Made Just For You

» ——→•←—— «

Jeremiah 29:11 says, " 'For I know the plans I have for you,' declares the Lord, 'plans to prosper you, and not to harm you, plans to give you hope and a future.' " (NIV) God has a plan for each of us. Our journey through life has been custom made just for us! He has plans for us that are beyond our wildest dreams! It is up to us to stay the course. Your weight-loss journey has been uniquely designed just for you and only you. The challenges you may face are used to build your stamina for the greater things ahead and reveal a finished product that is pleasing to God. God has plans for you. Therefore, while on this journey, be encouraged when you face people and things that may cause you to question whether you can complete it. Tell yourself, "God has a perfect plan for me. I can and I will finish strong."

So, now that you know that God has a plan for you, don't be discouraged by others who may feel you should stop. They may tell you, "Girl you look good! Why are you still going to the gym? Is it that serious that you have to carry your lunch? One wing won't kill you!" Be mentally prepared to not allow the words of others to discourage you. Remember, this journey has been custom made for you. God has plans for you and He will be there every step of the way. You got this! Hang in there and stay focused on being a healthier, better you.

Tell yourself, "I am capable of reaching my goals and becoming healthier for life!"

Your Thoughts:

_____

_____

_____

_____

_____

_____

_____

_____

_____

_____

_____

_____

_____

_____

_____

_____

_____

_____

_____

_____

Day 7
You Don't Have To Live With It

Along your weight-loss journey, you will have times when everything is going well. You're making healthier food choices, your mindset is in check, you're getting your workouts in, your scale is moving in the right direction, etc. But then life happens…and it sends a curve ball to your journey. Whether it's issues at work, a family crisis, relationship issues, or just the pressure of the journey itself, interruption of progress has occurred. These issues can derail your journey and set you back. They can make you feel like you can't go on and keep you stuck in that dark place of hopelessness. When issues throw you off course, you may feel defeated and doubt your ability to get back up. Remember, you don't have to live with defeat and self-doubt. Today is a new day. You can rise again and start anew!

Today is the day you stop beating up yourself! It is time to get up, dust off defeat, doubt, worry, and any other thoughts that will keep you stagnant! Today is a new day! Isaiah 41:10 says, "So do not fear, for I am with you; do not be dismayed, for I am your God. I will strengthen you and help you; I will uphold you with my righteous right hand."(NIV) God gives us the power to get back up and start again! You have to believe that in spite of what you may have gone through, He will give you strength and help you become better than you were before! He will not let you fall. You don't have to stay in a place of defeat. You have the option to get up and fight again Use your setbacks as a setup for success! Setbacks can only strengthen you and make you stronger for the journey ahead. It is when you get back up and try again that you WIN.

Tell yourself, "I am a winner! My setbacks refine me and set me up for success. I am strength!"

Your Thoughts:

_____

_____

_____

_____

_____

_____

_____

_____

_____

_____

_____

_____

_____

_____

_____

_____

_____

_____

_____

_____

_____

Day 8
God, Are You There?

Have you ever had a day, week, month, or even a year that was full of challenges at every turn? So much coming at you at one time to the point you just wanted to give up, throw in the towel, lie in your bed, and forget about ever trying again?

These types of wilderness moments will make you wonder where God is. They may move you to ask, "God, are you there? Do you not see what I am going through?" As you move through your weight-loss journey, you may experience times when there are so many challenges that you want to revert back to old ways because your new ways are challenging and you may not see those quick results you're longing for. For instance, there's so much going on at work, with family, your mate, or that feeling of depression you're fighting to keep at bay. Days like this will have you forget about cooking your healthy meals and go to the drive-thru of your favorite fast food restaurant. These instances will challenge your ability to get off the couch, get dressed, and get your workout in. You may even sit there and wonder, "What's this all about? Why do I bother? Where is God in this situation?"

Be encouraged, Lady of Power! Joshua 1:9 says, "Have I not commanded you? Be strong and courageous. Do not be afraid; do not be discouraged, for the Lord your God will be with you wherever you go." (NIV) God is with you even in the moments when it seems He's so far away. It's in the toughest moments along the journey to weight-loss success that you have to remember that God will not leave you. He won't give up on you, no matter how challenging your situation may seem at that moment. God is testing your faith. He wants to know that you trust Him in good times and tough times. You have to keep the faith knowing that He's always there.

So, Lady of Power, don't let the challenges that life

may present get you off track. You're on your way to an amazing transformation, freedom and a new life of improved health and wellness. You can't afford to stop now! Your ability to stay the course to better health will transcend your own expectations.

It's time to shift your mindset and remember who your God is. Build your strength and your POWER daily by studying God's word. Surround yourself with scripture like Joshua 1:9 to remind you that God is with you every step you take on this journey. He's with you through every challenge, expecting you to trust Him! Lady of Power, He's building your stamina for the long haul. God wants you to be successful, strong, and faithful every day because He has a plan – a purpose for your life.

Tell yourself, "I am able to push through all of my challenges because I know God is with me every day. I will have the victory, no matter what! Amen."

Your Thoughts:

Day *9*
It's Time To Speak To Your Mountains!

》———▶•◀———《

Lady of Power, do you realize that the true power you possess will not only achieve weight-loss success but will achieve all of your heart's desires? Do you ever wonder why it seems so hard? Or, how do you release your power and achieve everything you've always wanted? Keep reading because today, you'll claim the victory. It's time to speak to your mountains!

Mark 11:23 says, " Truly I tell you, if anyone says to this mountain, 'Go throw yourself into the sea,' and does not doubt in their heart but believes that what they say will happen, it will be done for them." (NIV) It is time for you, Lady of Power, to speak to your mountains like never before. Your mountains are the thoughts in your mind which the enemy uses to make you feel that you can't be successful. When you doubt your ability to reach your weight-loss goals by saying, "I can't lose all this weight. I might as well give up because it's too hard. I don't have the ability to be strong and eat right. I might as well be fat and happy, rather than go through this! I've been here before and failed; there's no hope." or "I just can't do this. I am not ready!" you are allowing yourself to be defeated before you begin. You are saying, "No." to a healthier YOU.

Don't you know that God has created you for a unique purpose? Do you know that God has a plan for your life that exceeds your expectations? All you have to do is trust in His power! You have to know wholeheartedly that He has given you the power to speak to your mountains. It's time to believe in your heart without any doubt that you can tell your mountains to go jump into the sea! Today, you will tell your mountains to leave. Tell those self-doubting thoughts that they don't reside in your mind anymore. Lady of Power, make a commitment daily to speak to your mountains by letting them know they're no longer welcome to set up shop in your mind. Send them on their way!

Lady of Power, now that you have spoken to and cleared your mountains, it's time to welcome God's love. Inviting God's love in means, with open arms, you invite positive thoughts to reside in your mind. These positive thoughts will fill you with daily belief in what you have the ability to do along this transformation journey. God has created you to be a Lady of Power; spirit-filled, Godly, smart, beautiful, and capable of achieving success in every area of your life.

If you believe that God has empowered you with the ability to speak to your mountains, then you have to claim it! You have to believe that you can become healthy and fit like never before. Every day, speak those positive thoughts to continuously keep out those mountains. Tell yourself, "I will overcome my health challenges. I'm capable and equipped for success on my journey. I can lose weight. I'm a WINNER on this journey."

Now walk in it! Lady of Power, stay prayerful, repeat daily positive thoughts, and watch – with God's help – those mountains throw themselves into the sea!

Your Thoughts:

_____

_____

_____

_____

_____

_____

_____

_____

_____

_____

_____

_____

_____

_____

_____

_____

_____

_____

_____

_____

_____

Day *10*
You Owe It To Him*!*

The journey to weight-loss success can seem like an unreachable goal to accomplish as you strive each day to stay the course. You may even ask yourself, "Why am I putting my body through this?" You go week to week, determined to eat healthier and get your workouts in, praying each time it gets easier. In your mind, you may even ask, "What is this all for anyway? Maybe I need to just accept myself the way I am."

Well, Lady of Power, hold on to your seat because you're about to read a powerful message about why you MUST press forward to get your body in the best health and shape possible.

1 Corinthians 6:19 says, "Do you not know that your bodies are temples of the Holy Spirit, who is in you,

whom you have received from God? You are not your own." (NIV). You have heard this scripture read several times, but let's apply it to your weight-loss journey.

When you MAKE a decision to give your life to Christ and become a Christian, the Holy Spirit moves in, and therefore, is now residing in you! At that very moment your body becomes God's temple, it no longer belongs to you. This means, you're no longer authorized to do as you please with your body.

Lady of Power, your body is God's holy temple designed for a specific purpose! Therefore, you owe it to God to stay the course and get His temple in order. Clean His temple by shifting your mindset. You must get your body ready to carry out His purpose by keeping the mountains out of the way so that you can see His vision and share a good word to the people He has assigned to you! You must eat healthier and make time for fitness so that you're physically ready to withstand the tough journey. You owe it to HIM!

Lady of Power, don't miss God's purpose for your

life because you're not committed to staying the course and taking care of His temple! Take care of your body so that you don't disrupt God's purpose for you. Each time you find it challenging to turn away food that's not the best choice, such as fried wings and french fries, or you're skipping workouts because you're tired or just not motivated enough, tell yourself, "I must take care of God's temple! I must push through so that I can be used for God's purpose for my life!" Shout if you have to, "I will NOT disrupt God's purpose for me!"

You can do this. You owe it to God. You owe this journey to a healthier lifestyle to yourself! Now walk in it!

Your Thoughts:

Day *11*
Stick To Your Power Plan By Staying Focused For Success!

》———▶·◀———《

Have you ever left work determined to hit the gym, only to decide to get off at the mall exit for an outfit you wanted? Have you ever made a decision to go out with girlfriends over the weekend and didn't make time to plan your meals? Have you cooked for the week, but decided to eat out with friends for lunch? Or were you supposed to go to the gym, but found sitting at home, socializing on social media a better option?

Can you relate to any of these questions? Proverbs 4:25 says, "Let your eyes look straight ahead; fix your gaze directly before you." (NIV). Lady of Power, it's time to stick to your Power Plan by staying focused on success. You've made a decision to make a lifestyle change. Whether you created a plan with a trainer, or a Power Plan with the Mind, Body, & Power Coach, or made your own plan for success – you must stay focused. In Proverbs, this verse talks about being "sold out" to your journey. This is not the time to let distractions prevent you from seeing the success of your dedication and perseverance.

Be vigilant over your spirit. Avoid temptations, whether from peers, family, or your mind. Be careful not to let others, or self-sabotaging behaviors, derail what God has allowed you to create for a successful journey. Keep your focus on the end result! As the scripture says, "...fix your gaze directly before you." You already know that God created you for a purpose. Stick to your Power Plan and watch how your success grows each day!

Lady of Power, God will be pleased with your ability to stay focused. Let His Spirit speak to your mind so that you can keep your eye straight ahead and WIN. Tell yourself, "I am destined for success. I am focused on the WIN."

Your Thoughts:

_____

_____

_____

_____

_____

_____

_____

_____

_____

_____

_____

_____

_____

_____

_____

_____

_____

_____

_____

_____

_____

Day *12*
What Drives You?

≫—➤•◀—≪

Have you ever wondered why it seems challenging to meet your weight-loss goals? Did you ever take a moment to ask yourself what it would take to fully commit?

Lady of Power, take a moment and fetch a sheet of paper. Reflect for a moment on what your top five reasons are for being on this weight-loss journey – with number one being your most important reason. Next, read them carefully, and as you read them, feel free to reorder them from the most important to the least important.

Good! Now, let's talk about how important these reasons are to your journey. The reasons you wrote down have to be things you're truly passionate about achieving on this journey to a healthier you. If you're passionate about those things, you'll do what it takes to be successful. You'll develop plans, strategies, seek help, and make a decision that you're on this journey for the long haul.

Lady of Power, after looking at your reasons, can you truly say, "I'm driven by these reasons, I want success so bad that I'm willing to do what's necessary to achieve my weight-loss goals."? You have to know what drives you on this journey. What's your purpose for wanting to be healthy and fit? If you don't have a clear picture of what drives you on this journey – your real purpose – you won't stay committed. You won't want it bad enough to push through the challenges that come along this journey to better health and fitness.

Take time to really reflect on what it is that drives you on this journey. Write it down. Make it clear and concise so that you know why it's important to you. For example, if your reason is to get off of high blood pressure medication so that you can extend your life and live the life which God has purposed you for, then this becomes the driving force behind your journey. All you can see in front of you is getting off those medications for good! You want to see that change so bad that you're willing to give up salty food, cook healthy meals at home, create a workout plan each week, and be mindful of self-sabotaging behaviors. You are built for this!

It's time to be honest and dig deep and find what drives you on this journey – that is, if you don't already know. If you do know, you've been charged to stay with the process and not let anything stop YOU. Writing down your reasons will help to keep you focused on how important this is in your life. Your journey – your testimony to weight-loss success – may help someone else who is trying to make a decision to start. You have to have a clear vision and know what drives you so that you will be able to testify how God has brought you through this journey. Do you know that your testimony can leave an impact that could affect future generations? Habakkuk 2:2 says, "Then the Lord answered me and said: 'Write the vision, And make it plain on tablets, That he may run who reads it.' " (NKJV) Your journey is not just about you. It's also about how God can use your journey in years to come to help others that have heard about your success. Know what drives you so that you can please God along this journey. Seek answers from God through prayer and scriptures so that your journey changes your life and others'.

Tell yourself, "I will be honest with myself about what really drives me on this journey. I have a purpose and a vision for success!"

Your Thoughts:

_____

_____

_____

_____

_____

_____

_____

_____

_____

_____

_____

_____

_____

_____

_____

_____

_____

_____

_____

_____

_____

Day *13*
It's Time To Plan & Execute For Success!

≫——➤•◀——≪

Do you know what it takes to start and maintain your weight-loss journey? Have you taken some time to sit and put your pen to paper to decide what you will need to get started? Do you have a routine in place to keep you on track for success? These are important questions to use to evaluate your readiness for the journey. Lady of Power, if you haven't done so already, it's time to create and execute your plans for weight-loss success!

Today, as you either design your plan for the journey or evaluate the one you already have in place, be encouraged, knowing that God is walking with you through the process. You're not planning alone. Having a plan in place and executing that plan with fidelity will equal lasting success! So, you may be wondering why a plan is so important and how it really leads to success.

Proverbs 21:5 says, "The plans of the diligent lead to profit as surely as haste leads to poverty." (NIV) Lady of Power, you must be diligent in your planning. You must be determined to make a change for the betterment of your health. You must be willing to step out of your comfort zone to execute your new plan for weight-loss success! As God's word says, "...the plans of the diligent lead to profit..." Therefore, you already have confirmation that your diligence in planning for your transformation will equal your profit – which is good health. If you don't plan for your journey, you won't achieve your desired results. So be careful of shortcuts that only lead to temporary success!

Lady of Power, you may be thinking, "Well, what should my plan look like? What does a routine look like?" Or just plain and simple, "How do I start?" These are great questions! First and foremost, before you sit down and plan, take a moment to pray and ask God to give you guidance as you begin creating your plan. Next, get out your planner, notebook/journal, pens, highlighters, or whatever else you believe will be essential to your planning process.

Your plan should consist of a journal where you not only write about the journey, but where you document your start date, current weight, height, age, and measurements (optional). In addition, your journal entry should include your long-term goal weight, as well as your short-term goals for each week. A coach who specializes in weight-loss is helpful in this process of planning. In this journal, you can keep your meal plan (if you don't have one, seek your coach, trainer, or nutritionist for guidance) or have a separate book where you plan your meals and create your weekly grocery lists. This process is crucial because food is 85% of the weight-loss process, and exercise is the other 15%. Therefore, you need to create a routine for ensuring that your meals will be prepared each week. In addition, create a weekly schedule for the days you will work out. Make sure you select days and times that are realistic to your schedule so that you have time for your family and other life events.

Lady of Power, you can do this! Make time each day to pray, read your Lady of Power book daily to stay inspired and positive, and surround yourself with people who will uplift you. Planning is crucial to your transformation success. Therefore, create your plan and execute it so that you can live a healthier life and do all the things that God has preordained for you. Tell yourself, "I am a planner and I have the ability to create a plan that I can execute to achieve weight-loss success!"

Your Thoughts:

Day *14*
Dare To Be The Most Powerful You!

》———➤·◄———《

Have you ever sat and thought about all of the possibilities for your life and it scared you to death? You sat there thinking about all of your gifts, talents, business ideas, and in some cases the ministry that God has revealed to you. At that moment you smile, you dream, you visualize yourself fully accomplishing those goals. But then, the thought of doing it scares you to the point that you retreat, become scared, afraid, and doubtful of the possibilities of a new, improved, and transformed YOU.

Lady of Power that same doubt, those fears, and those scary feelings will keep you from accomplishing your weight-loss goals. It may not be every day, but those limiting thoughts, keep you from tapping into your ability to become your best self. Limiting beliefs keep you from reaching your maximum potential. What you tell yourself can either propel you into your destiny or keep you stuck in the same place. But today, dare yourself to be the strongest YOU.

It's a new day and a new you! Dare yourself to add more faith in your life. Walk in faith knowing that whatever is in your heart to accomplish, God will walk every step with you to see it to fruition. He wants you to be the healthiest you. He wants you to carry out the assignment He has created you for on this earth. Now is your time to step up boldly, by exercising not just your body, but your mind. Lady of Power, you were built with amazing faith. No longer are you to be afraid of the endless possibilities of living an amazing, healthy life.

Hebrews 11:1 says, "Now faith is confidence in what we hope for and assurance about what we do not see." (NIV) This scripture tells you that all you have to do is have faith in God's process. The things you desire and see in your dreams or visions should not scare you; be faithful in knowing that God will prevail. He will reward you for trusting in what He will do for your life, even when it's not physically in front of you.

On your weight-loss journey thus far, you have visualized yourself a healthier you, full of energy, and physically fit. You have visualized yourself in that new sexy dress that makes heads turn. You may have even dreamed of finally being introduced to the new love of your life! Lady of Power, don't let these visions scare you and cause you not to have faith in what God will do to help you live a healthy and rewarding life! Dare yourself to push forward and let your dreams be the driving force behind your amazing transformation.

Look in the mirror, and tell yourself, "I am not afraid of being the most powerful ME. God wants me to have a healthy and amazing life!"

Your Thoughts:

Day *15*
Get On Track. Get Your Focus Back!
(Acknowledge Your Pattern, Stop The Cycle.)

》——➤•◂——《

Are you tired of starting your weight-loss journey over and over again? Do you keep saying, "This is the last time I'm going to start over."? Are you making excuses for starting? Are you finally ready to get focused, acknowledge your patterns, self-sabotaging behaviors, and end the "on the wagon, off the wagon" cycle?

Lady of Power, the enemy doesn't want you to be successful, but God wants the best for you. He needs you to get focused so that you can transform your life by living healthy and also empower others who need to see that the impossible is possible!! Amen! It's time to get "real" with yourself! What patterns do you repeat that keep you on the vicious dieting cycle of being "on the wagon, off the wagon"? Lady of Power, it's time to acknowledge your pattern and stop the cycle!

Today, take inventory of your attempts at living a healthier lifestyle. Take out a sheet of paper, fold it in half, and jot down the top five things or habits that are impeding your journey. These are the things that keep you on the dieting cycle. These are the patterns of behavior that keep manifesting every time you start. What seems to get you off track and cause you to lose focus? Acknowledge it today. Be totally honest.

Now, on the other side of the paper, jot down reasonable ways to address these issues when they arise. Take time to really think deeply about how you and the Holy Spirit can create a strategy to keep you going when the items you listed start rearing their ugly heads. For example, perhaps one of your habits is going hard on the journey to the point that you're so extreme, you reach burnout.

Here's an example of going hard on the journey. When you first start out, you're hitting the gym every day. In addition, you impose your new lifestyle habits on everyone, to the point that everything you discuss is all about your workout and weight-loss regimen. You're so strict with your food regimen – which is not a bad thing – but it's to the point where your friends and family don't want to invite you to functions because you've made it clear to them that you have no balance. This may sound a little familiar. Lady of Power, this is self-sabotage! You are setting yourself up for burnout. When you reach burnout, you've exhausted your body and mind to a point that you have no power to keep going. Now you fall off the wagon and it sometimes takes weeks and months to get back on track.

So, Lady of Power, be mindful of the things that impede your journey. God wants you to be successful in all things. Acknowledge the pattern, seek Him, and ask Him for guidance. Even if it means sending you the help you need (a coach) to make this new journey to weight-loss success a lasting one. Please know that God will uplift you and do more than you ask. He knows your needs before you ask, but God wants you to acknowledge that you need His help to end the cycle that's delaying your weight-loss success. Take a moment to meditate on this scripture to remind you that God's grace will manifest itself on your journey in ways beyond your expectations. Ephesians 3:20-21 says, "Now to him who is able to do immeasurably more than all we ask or imagine, according to his power that is at work within us, to him be glory…" (NIV) Lady of Power, give God the glory in advance for what He's getting ready to do for you on this journey to a healthier you! Know that with the help of the Holy Spirit, you'll be able to develop a sound plan of action to combat the things that keep you "off the wagon" and step into a place where "on the wagon" is where you'll stay! Are you excited? Now it's time to walk this journey and get ready for all of the blessings you'll receive along the way. No matter how hard it may seem, embrace the unexpected and celebrate the smallest accomplishments!

Lady of Power, take a moment and tell yourself, "I love me – the imperfect, perfect, me. I have the ability to end the dieting cycle and create habits that will not impede my progress as I work to change my lifestyle. I am ready for all that God will send my way! Amen."

Your Thoughts:

Day *16*
Even God Has A Rest Day.
Relax, Relate, & Release!

≫——▸•◂——≪

Have you been so fired up on your journey that you haven't taken a day to relax, relate, and release? Do you have an "I can't stop, won't stop" motto? Do you find it hard to carve out some downtime?

If you have nodded, "yes." to any of the above questions, it's time to find a place and time to rest. On this journey to weight-loss success, you have to create balance. You don't want to overwhelm yourself to the point you quit because you have exhausted yourself to no end. Genesis 2:2 says, "By the seventh day God had finished the work he had been doing; so on the seventh day he rested from all his work." (NIV) Even God set aside a day to rest from work. You have to do the same.

At times, downtime can be a challenge because you want so badly to see success. You begin to develop blinders that are cemented in your mind to the point that your weight-loss journey becomes obsessive! Yes obsessive! You eat, sleep, and breathe the weight-loss journey. You cut off friends, you don't take the time to socialize because you haven't developed the ability to cope in normal settings when it comes to food. On the other hand, sometimes because you are afraid of failure, you may totally avoid any event or socializing that may cause you to buckle under pressure.

You may even superimpose your journey on family and friends who may not be where you are, causing them to exile you from functions. Yes, this happens and you won't even know until later. Create a workout plan that makes sense. You don't have to spend seven days in the gym to get results. Be reasonable with yourself. Select three or four days that you will dedicate to working out. Prepare your meals each week. Also, schedule fun activities with family and friends. Get rid of obsessive behaviors that will leave you burnt out and no longer enthusiastic about your weight-loss journey. God needs you to go all the way and meet success!

Lady of Power, make time to relax, relate, and release! This journey is yours, so enjoy it. Tell yourself, "I am important. I will make time to enjoy my journey to a healthier me."

Your Thoughts:

_____
_____
_____
_____
_____
_____
_____
_____
_____
_____
_____
_____
_____
_____
_____
_____
_____
_____
_____
_____

Day *17*
You Have The P.O.W.E.R.

≫——➤·◀——≪

Lady of Power, do you know that you have the P. O. W. E. R. to make what you thought was impossible...possible? Have you begun to understand that you have the P.O.W.E.R. to defy the odds by trusting God to walk with you on this journey to a lifestyle makeover? Matthew 19:26 says, "Jesus looked at them and said, 'With man this is impossible, but with God all things are possible.' " (NIV) God is the giver of life. He sent His son, Jesus, who died for your sins so that you may be given another chance to the life He has designed for you. God does not want you to fail. You must remember daily that trusting God is the key to changing the impossible to possible, even when people don't believe! The power lies in you!

Let's take a moment and explore the acronym for P.O.W.E.R.:

P is for Purpose. God's Spirit lives in you. Therefore, He created you to carry out a specific purpose on this earth. If you take time to allow the Spirit to reign in your life and move out of your own way, God will handle your challenges along the journey. You must understand that God wants you to achieve your life's purpose. When you develop an intimate relationship with God, your purpose will become clear. You will walk proudly and work hard to take care of your body, so that you can carry out your purpose. God will give you the stamina to push along the journey to a healthier you!

O is for Obedience. God smiles when you make a decision to be obedient to His will. In the New Testament, it talks about how you display your love for Christ by being obedient in all things. Are you being obedient to God's will for you? Are staying committed to your weight-loss goals so that you can be a great example of how God rewards obedience? When you are obedient, you show reverence to God by following and staying true to His word, commandments, and instructions – His will. On your journey to weight-loss success, you can WIN if you listen carefully to the whispers of God. He provides instructions for you to help you not abandon the process. Obedience is one of the keys to never getting back on the dieting cycle.

W is for Woman. Lady of Power, do you know that you are a special person? You have been uniquely designed to withstand challenges and situations that men could never withstand. You're the caretaker of your home, created to ensure that all who have been given to you are nurtured, loved, and cared for daily. As a woman, you please God because of your ability to take on so many responsibilities and almost never buckle under the pressure. You just handle it. As a woman who is pressing forward to become healthier and meet your weight-loss goals, you are breaking generational curses. Lady of Power, you are giving the next generation a chance at a healthy future because you're implementing a healthier lifestyle for your family. When you create a healthier lifestyle, you instill in your family the values of being healthier. They extend this knowledge to their families, thus creating a healthier world to carry out their purpose! This generational shift pleases God.

E is for Endurance. Endurance can be defined as you having the ability to withstand tough or adverse situations or conditions. Lady of Power, you are built for this journey! God has created you with the ability to make changes in your diet and increase your exercise. Remember the Old Testament story of Job? He endured so many situations, from his body being stricken with illness, to him losing everything he worked for, even losing his family, but God rewarded him in the end. God rewarded Him for his endurance and faith in the process. He had a "no matter what!" type of attitude.

It is time for you to develop a "no matter what!" attitude. Your weight-loss transformation requires you to endure changing of your food that may not initially satisfy your palate. You may have days when your body doesn't want to go the extra mile at the gym. Endure and see your results of being faithful and dedicated to what God is doing in this process. Endurance increases your discipline factor. You will see that you'll become more disciplined when you make a decision that no matter what, you will push through.

R is for Resilience. Lady of Power, it means that you possess the "bounce back" ability. No matter what situations or challenges you may face on this journey, you have the ability to demonstrate your resilience. You are like an elastic band. No matter how that band is stretched or bent, it returns to its natural state! That's you! This capability lies within you. 2 Timothy 1:7 says, "For the Spirit God gave us does not make us timid, but gives us power, love and self-discipline." (NIV) Lady of Power, you are designed for this journey to weight-loss success. God gives you the power to be stretched and bent, but never broken. Amen! Do not be afraid of the process because it seems hard. This is for you. It's when you're stretched that you grow with God and you increase your "bounce back" ability.

Tell yourself, "I possess the P.O.W.E.R. to make this journey to a healthier me happen. I have a "no matter what" attitude, therefore, I have "bounce back" ability! I have the P.O.W.E.R.!"

Your Thoughts:

Day *18*
Grab Hold of Your Confidence & Persevere!

>>———➤•◄———《

Take a moment and see if you can answer these questions. What is confidence? What does it mean to be confident? What role does confidence have in your weight-loss journey? And what's the connection between confidence and perseverance? Lady of Power, get comfortable, center yourself, and be ready to be inspired today - to grab hold of your confidence and persevere!

So what is confidence? Confidence is a feeling of self-assurance that comes from your belief in your own abilities and qualities. It's your ability to believe in your inner you and the gifts and talents which God has uniquely blessed you with from birth. Your confidence level is crucial to your weight-loss journey. Your ability to recognize that you have what it takes to achieve your weight-loss goals will propel you to heights that exceed what you expected. It's time to grab hold of your confidence. It's in you! Dig deep, pull from within, and you will find that you have more confidence than you think!

Do not doubt for a moment that your confidence is a part of this journey to healthier you! God needs you to have confidence in your journey. In addition, He wants you to rely on Him to see you through this process. God wants you to call on Him on those days when your confidence might fall. He is looking for you to grab hold of your confidence and persevere!

Hebrews 10:35-36 says, "So do not throw away your confidence; it will be richly rewarded. You need to persevere so that when you have done the will of God, you will receive what He has promised." (NIV) Lady of Power, your confidence in your abilities and qualities which God has blessed you with will allow you to walk this journey every day. When you couple your confidence with perseverance, you are now able to take your journey to the next level!

Perseverance is your ability to have unyielding faith. It's your ability to push through all circumstances, block out limiting beliefs, and achieve what some may see as impossible! Lady of Power, now is the time to grab hold of your confidence and persevere. God wants to reward you for making your health a priority by staying on the journey. Take hold of your confidence in your ability to let go of unhealthy food choices, no longer self-sabotage your journey, and exercise to get your body in shape.

Tell yourself, "I am able to grab hold of my confidence and persevere on this journey to weight-loss success. I am ready for God to bless me every step of the way, for my faith is in His Power!"

Your Thoughts:

_____

_____

_____

_____

_____

_____

_____

_____

_____

_____

_____

_____

_____

_____

_____

_____

_____

_____

_____

_____

_____

Day *19*
Body Power For Every Step of Your Journey

$\gg\!\!\longrightarrow\!\cdot\blacktriangleleft\!\longrightarrow\!\ll$

Have you ever had moments where you struggle to look in a full-length mirror at your body? Have you avoided the full-length mirror because it was hard to come to grips with the fact that you haven't taken care of yourself? Or have you lost some of the weight because of your new lifestyle commitment, but still can't look in the mirror? Lady of Power, today and every day after you read this inspiration, you will leave those thoughts behind! It's time to claim your body power for every step of your journey.

This may be a hard concept to digest right away and you may need to read this inspiration a few times before it really sinks in, but you must change how you see yourself physically, whether it's the beginning of the journey, the middle, or your final stage. You may not be satisfied with what you see right now, but avoiding mirrors and thinking or saying unkind things about your body doesn't help the process. You must love yourself and speak positive words over your body daily. If you are unable to love your body along the journey, you will project that energy to others as well. It's like the old saying, "If you can't love yourself, how do you expect others to love you?"

Here's a scripture to reflect on each time you have unkind thoughts come to mind about your body. Psalm 100:3 says, "Know that the Lord is God. It is he who made us, and we are his; we are his people, the sheep of his pasture." (NIV) God made you in a unique way. There are no copies of you! God made you, He loves you, and He wants you to love the woman He has created. God's love for you is sufficient for you to realize that you must love your body, regardless of where you are on your journey. God has unconditional love for you! Therefore, not loving your body is like telling God that you are not pleased with what He created. It's time to take your power and improve God's temple. He built your body for a purpose. You were uniquely designed to carry out an assignment. It's time to use your body power for every step of the journey.

Lady of Power, you may be wondering "How do I accomplish this?" In order to use your body power for every step of the journey, you must keep your mind in the right space. You have to always remember that God is always with you, the Holy Spirit resides in you, and will guide you each and every day. It's up to you to continuously remind yourself that you are God's greatest creation. He created you with a powerful purpose. Having the right mindset will power you from your inside to your outside. You must walk in your power like never before, knowing that your current body is being refined daily. Your body is your temporary look; it's under construction. Think of it like this, when companies make a decision to renovate a facility, as they plan, begin, and while they move throughout the process, they remain hopeful and excited because of what the end result will be.

Lady of Power, you must develop the same mindset when it comes to your body! Plan by getting the right mindset, preparing your meals, and organizing your schedule to get your body in shape. Next, work daily to execute your plan to the fullest. Love yourself, smile, and walk in your power every day. You must remain hopeful and excited because God has created a beautiful body and the new look will be even more fabulous! Body power – claim it every step of the journey!

Now, look in that mirror, a full-length mirror, and tell yourself, "I have the body power for every step of the journey. I love me. I am God's greatest creation."

Your Thoughts:

Day *20*
You Control The Food, Not the Food Control You!

Have you ever felt like you didn't have control over your finances, relationships, job situations, or even your children? Maybe there have been instances where these things have controlled your life to the extent of believing there's no hope. Food can become the escape from life's issues and seem to provide comfort in those times when everything else may be out of control. But do you know that the food you eat for comfort also controls you? This is called emotional eating. Emotional eating is when you react to life's events by overindulging in food. As a result, now the food is also controlling you. Whether it's a happy moment, sad moment, or a "just because" moment, these moments become reasons to eat. Hence, weight gain and other health problems arise. Today, Lady of Power, be encouraged. You have the ability to control the food, not let the food control you.

You have made a decision to live a healthier lifestyle and break free from the things that control you, as well as make your weight-loss success a reality. Continue to water your mind with positive thinking, arm yourself with God's word, and recognize the self-sabotaging behaviors that will keep you on the dieting cycle. 1 Peter 5:8 says, "Be alert and of sober mind. Your enemy the devil prowls around like a roaring lion looking for someone to devour. Resist him, standing firm in the faith, because you know that the family of believers throughout the world is undergoing the same kind of sufferings."(NIV) Lady of Power, you have the ability to remain in control on this journey and WIN.

As the scripture says, "Be alert and of sober mind." There are challenges that will come your way and will seek to test your ability to practice self-control or maintain your willpower to resist the urges to stay on track! Be vigilant and recognize the challenge in front of you. Stand strong and have faith knowing that this challenge is not worth you turning to food to solve it.

You can make it. You will make it. Don't let the enemy win! Stand on your faith in God, knowing that He will prevail and bring you through every challenging moment. Remember, He has given you the ability to control the food, not the other way round!

Now, Lady of Power, stand strong and poised and look in the mirror and tell yourself, "I have control over my food. It doesn't control me. I declare victory over every food challenge! I will make choices that help me reach my weight-loss goals. In Jesus name, Amen."

Your Thoughts:

Day *21*
You Can't Get Through This Journey Without God

»———➤•◄———«

Have you ever tried to accomplish something, but couldn't without help? Have you ever wondered why your journey to weight-loss freedom seems very challenging when doing it on your own? Have you made God an intricate part of your journey? Have you truly made time for God?

Lady of Power, the time is now, if God is not a part of your daily walk on this weight-loss journey, then the burden may be too much. Your results will be minimal if God is not an intricate part of your life. You can't get through this journey without God. He is the most essential part of your journey. You will need Him every step of the way. Your spiritual connection with God will allow Him to speak to you in not only good times but also during those difficult times. There will be moments when family and friends can't say anything that will help you push through, but having God along the journey will allow the Holy Spirit that lives in you to speak to you when you need it the most.

In those times when you think weight-loss success is impossible because so many of life's challenges get in the way, take a moment and reflect on this scripture found in Psalm 73:26, "My flesh and my heart may fail, but God is the strength of my heart and my portion forever." (NIV) This journey would not be worth it if it were easily achieved. You have to go through some peaks and some valleys to have a testimony – a story of how God strengthens you. This scripture is a reminder that we will be tested and at times fail along the way, but God gives you the power (strength) to always get back up. He is always there for you, forever. With the aid of the Holy Spirit, you can and will get through this transformation process.

Laugh at your challenges, even when it's hard to

accept some of the things which seek to suck the very life out of you. No matter who abandons you along this journey, God is always there! Take time daily to access His help through prayer, meditation, and scriptures. Remember, "No cross, no crown!" Let God in, accept your assignment, seek Him for guidance and understanding, cry, laugh, and keep fighting, no matter how hard the journey gets. God has an exciting future for you; you have to be fit for the journey so that you can serve the people He has assigned to you.

Lady of Power, look in the mirror and tell yourself, "I can get through this journey because He is always with me. I am strong and capable of meeting my weight-loss goals and be the living example of God's greatness! Amen."

Your Thoughts:

_____

_____

_____

_____

_____

_____

_____

_____

_____

_____

_____

_____

_____

_____

_____

_____

_____

_____

_____

_____

Day *22*
Have Faith In The Process

≫——➤•◄——≪

So you have made a decision to eat healthier, go to the gym, or get a trainer! This decision requires you to make some lifestyle shifts that may not be comfortable in the beginning. You may even question whether it's worth doing. You may feel this is too hard, too frustrating, too restricting, and not for you. Right?

Well, Lady of Power, it's time to have faith in the process! Everything you set your mind to achieve, whether it's a degree, new job, new love, or adjusting finances – is a process. Losing weight is a process, too. Take a moment to reflect, way back, on a time when you had to learn how to ride a bike, adapt to a new job assignment, or anything else that was new. In order for you to become good at any of these, there was a process you had to go through. Once you went through this process, you could almost complete the task in your sleep! Your weight-loss journey is the same. Making the shift to a healthier lifestyle, for a lasting result, is a process. You have to be willing to persevere and endure on those tough days when you feel like you want to quit and revert back to old habits. It takes at least twenty-one days before something becomes a habit and almost six months before the new habit totally replaces the old habit. You have to have faith in yourself, and the power God gives you to have the courage to leave old habits behind and adopt new ones along the journey to a healthier YOU. Your ability to have faith in the process that God is bringing you through will yield you good health and much more.

Hebrews 10:36 says, "You need to persevere so that when you have done the will of God, you will receive what he has promised." (NIV) This process you are going through, whether you know it or not, is to glorify God's kingdom. This process is not just for you; it's for you to also do God's will. So, remember to be patient with the process. Better health equals your ability to further God's kingdom. Let Him use you! Have faith, knowing that He walks with you every step of your weight-loss journey.

Look in the mirror and tell yourself, "I will persevere and endure because this process is for my God! Amen!"

Your Thoughts:

Day *23*
Rejoice Along The Journey!

≫———➤·◄———≪

Have you ever felt that this journey is too much of a daunting task? Do you find that at times you overlook the small victories?

Lady of Power, this journey is like the turtle in the race. "Slow and steady wins the race!" This journey to weight-loss freedom is just that – "slow and steady". You have to have the mindset that you will be content with "slow and steady" progress. On this journey, you must be patient with the process. When you take the time to slowly, effectively, and steadily lose the weight, you will have time to learn what's working and what's not. You will have the opportunity to digest the process and let your body physically get acclimated to its new creation, day by day.

While on this slow but steady road to success, you have to make sure that you rejoice along the journey! You have to be sure to thank God for the big and small victories. Thank God and rejoice for the small victories like sticking to your meal plan for the week, to big ones like losing your first ten pounds! Or stepping out in that new dress that's a smaller size! Celebrate and rejoice along the journey! This is crucial to staying encouraged daily.

I Thessalonians 5:16-18 says, "Rejoice always, pray continually, give thanks in all circumstances; for this is God's will for you in Christ Jesus." (NIV) God wants us to rejoice along this journey in all things. He wants to intimately connect with you through prayer on this journey so that His Spirit can mold your mind and make it anew. As He makes it anew, He is allowing you to develop your power within to know that you can make it on this journey, in spite of whatever comes your way. God wants you to know that no matter what you experience, you must rejoice as a display of your faith in what He will do through Christ.

Rejoice along the journey! Tell yourself, "I will

rejoice for all things. I am faithful!"

Your Thoughts:

Day *24*
You Have To Be All The Way In

≫——➤·◄——≪

Have you found it difficult at times to stay committed to your weight-loss journey because you are still holding on to bad habits? Do you struggle with letting go of old habits for fear that life may not be what you consider normal?

Lady of Power, it's time to say, "Yes!" for real! Today is the day, if you have not completely done so yet, to let go of old habits that do not line up with your journey. It is time to say, "Yes!" and grant yourself a complete fresh start. Saying "Yes!" for real, means letting go of habits that do not equal your success. Be encouraged, because in letting go of old habits, renewing your mind, and physically taking care of your body, you're showing God that you're all the way in. Now let His process begin.

Let's take a look at 2 Corinthians 5:17 which says, "Therefore, if anyone is in Christ, he is a new creation. The old has passed away; behold, the new has come." (ESV) This scripture tells you that when you give your life to Christ, change your mindset, desire to live a life more pleasing to God, and say, "Yes!" for real, He grants you a fresh start. The things you did before you gave, or when you gave, your life to Christ are all forgiven. You have the opportunity to be born again, brand new, shiny, clean, forgiven, and ready to receive God's blessings. You are saying "Yes!" to wanting to live a Godly life. You understand that there will be challenges as well as triumphs, but you know that through Christ, you have the power to survive and can always come to Him when in need. What a great reward!

So, you may be wondering how all of this relates to the weight-loss journey. Lady of Power, think of your weight-loss journey as the moment you decided to give your life to Christ and become a woman of God. When you decided to make up your mind, step out in faith, change your eating habits, and get fit, you became a new creation. When you trust in God and make up your mind that you are sick and tired of being sick and tired, and when you desire a total change, and say, "Yes!" for real, your old habits become things of the past! Through the Spirit, you develop strategies against temptation, and no longer allow self-sabotaging behaviors and self-limiting beliefs to reign in your life. You become sold out and dedicated to living a healthier lifestyle.

Lady of Power, declare, "I am all the way in. I am sold out and dedicated to transforming my life and to living healthier!"

Your Thoughts:

_____

_____

_____

_____

_____

_____

_____

_____

_____

_____

_____

_____

_____

_____

_____

_____

_____

_____

_____

_____

Day *25*
Hold On, Your Weight-Loss Breakthrough Is Coming!

≫——➤·◄——≪

The journey that you're on is not for the weak! It is for the strong, the bold, and the warriors for Christ! Don't let the enemy make you feel that you can't make it on this journey. Make the devil a liar! Stand boldly and exemplify what faith in the process looks like. Hold on Lady of Power, because your breakthrough is on its way. You MUST stay the course so that you can receive all that God has in store for you.

1 Corinthians 10:13 says, "No temptation has overtaken you that is not common to man. God is faithful, and he will not let you be tempted beyond your ability, but with the temptation he will also provide the way of escape, that you may be able to endure it." (ESV) If we cleave to God, even in the toughest situations, God

will deliver us. God knows what we can bear and will only allow what He knows we have the strength to endure to come our way. But if we have faith in what our God can do in our circumstances and take refuge in Him, it's in that moment that our breakthroughs will take place. You must not allow the self-doubting words or pictures that the enemy paints or speaks to you cause you to forget that God's got you, every step of the way.

So when the days on the journey are going well and progress is being made, but the temptation to stop by your favorite fast food restaurant to celebrate rears its ugly head, be strong, stop and recognize the enemy, and keep driving! Breakthrough is coming and you MUST stand in your power knowing that God is able and He is watching. He wants to see how much you believe in His ability to set you free from emotional eating, self-sabotaging behaviors, lack of self-confidence, depression, and any other problems that food seems to be your way of solving.

If you are having one of those days when everything seems to be going wrong and you are struggling to stay on track, then know that your breakthrough is coming. If feelings of despair fill your mind and you feel like you want to give up and be content with where you are...your BREAKTHROUGH is on its way. And if nothing that anyone says at this point can heal your heart, know your BREAKTHROUGH is on its way!! Hold on! God is preparing you for your victory!

As the scripture says, "...but with the temptation he will also provide the way of escape, that you may be able to endure it." Lady of Power, stay the course, endure, and push through – knowing your escape is coming! You won't have a testimony about your journey to a healthier life if you don't go through triumphs and challenges! You see, the challenges we face on this journey to weight-loss success make us strong for the purpose God has set for us before we were born. When you abandon the journey early because you haven't made a total commitment to be "sold out" to the process, you will miss the blessings on the other side of the breakthrough! POWERFUL! Hold on! God will test you to see how faithful you are to HIM. Do you trust Him? How bad do you want to be healthy? Are you open for Him to use you in this process as an example of His faithfulness? Will your stated faith and actions line up?

Lady of Power, tell yourself, "My BREAKTHROUGH is on its way and I want it. I can endure the course! Amen."

Your Thoughts:

Day *26*
Renew Your Mind, Ignite Complete Transformation!

Lady of Power, are you ready for your complete transformation? If you answered, "Yes!" then keep reading, because today we are going to ignite complete transformation!!

Romans 12:2 says, "Do not conform to the pattern of this world, but be transformed by the renewing of your mind. Then you will be able to test and approve what God's will is – his good, pleasing and perfect will." (NIV) Are you ready to be that public demonstration of what happens when you align your thinking with God's Word? It is expected that as you read these Mind, Body, & Power Inspirations, you are accessing a daily opportunity to study God's word. God's word is designed to transform your life so that you live a life that is acceptable, good, and His perfect will!

In studying God's will, you learn how to live a righteous life. You become equipped to handle all situations because His Word has an answer for all things you experience in your everyday living. The more you stay in His Word, the more your mind will become renewed and move under the direction of the Spirit!

Lady of Power, you are uniquely designed to make a Godly mark on this world in a manner that God designed just for you. Therefore, you have to stay grounded and stand on God's word. You can't be like everyone else. You have to lead by example for the unbelievers. Sometimes, it's hard to be the minority when the majority is ruling and seeming to be doing well; while you strive to live according to God's will – whether it be taking care of His temple by walking away from those wings at a staff party or choosing not to date that man who you know is married. You know what I'm talking about, Lady of Power. You MUST decide to represent God's will.

What the world has deemed acceptable has caused

God's people to struggle to be the unicorn and follow God's will for our lives! You may be reading and thinking to yourself, "This is so hard to do at times. How do I not conform, and walk away in victory in Jesus' name?" As Paul shares in this scripture, the key to making God pleased is your decision not to go with the majority, but to choose to be "sold out" to God's will for your life. The power is in you.

As long as you make a serious commitment to studying God's word and operating in His will by practicing the teachings of the scriptures, you will experience a reset of your mindset! Therefore, no matter what you experience along your weight-loss journey, you know that you have the power to stand. You have God's word as a reference and an understanding that His word describes His perfect will for your life. God wants you to be your best.

Let's go even deeper...

Did you know this scripture also covers your physical body just as much as it does your mindset? In renewing our mindsets through the power of the Spirit, God also manifests this deliverance in your body. It's a part of the process when you align your thinking with God's word. So, now your body is a representation of an improved mindset towards life and the things we allow to enter our bodies! God is an awesome God!

These Mind, Body, and Power Inspirations are designed to do just what Paul describes in this scripture! Take a moment and say this to yourself, "I welcome the Spirit to change my mindset for a total transformation! I no longer want to go along with the majority. I am committed to being "sold out" for God and pleasing Him with my decisions!"

Your Thoughts:

_____

_____

_____

_____

_____

_____

_____

_____

_____

_____

_____

_____

_____

_____

_____

_____

_____

_____

_____

_____

_____

Day *27*
Today You Must Speak Strength

Lady of Power, today may be a day you want to find a secret space where you can escape from it all. Today may be a day when you feel you can't go on and nothing seems to be going as planned. The challenges of life are heavy and you may think to yourself, "How much more can one woman take?" If you are having these thoughts, please know that the challenges you face are all a part of God's process in molding you! Here is where you show God and yourself how faithful you really are to this process.

Today, Lady of Power, you must speak words of strength. Your words of strength are food to your mind and your body. Your words of strength keep you on the journey to a healthier you, because there's no room for you to tell yourself you can't. There's no room in your mind to let other people's decisions deter you from moving forward. Your words of strength don't allow your faith to waver when the odds are stacked against you as high as a one hundred-story skyscraper. If your boss tells you he's ending your contract, your words of strength will tell you, "No weapon formed against me shall prosper. (Isaiah 54:17) All things work together for my good. (Romans 8:28) New beginnings are on the way!" These words allow you the ability to get up and fight! If you ate poorly today, your words of strength will tell you, "I got this! I can get back on track and win this race to weight-loss success like never before!" If you or a family member are experiencing health issues, your words of strength will tell you, "Prayer changes things and by His stripes I am (they are) healed!" (Isaiah 53:5) Your words of strength are your POWER.

Psalm 18:32 says, "It is God who arms me with strength and makes my way perfect!" (NKJV) This scripture tells us that God gives us strength, which is your power. That power comes from studying His words. God's words speak life to any situation which you will face on your journey to weight-loss success. Your ability to use your words of strength will roll off your tongue as easily as you say your name because of your commitment to understanding God's words through the scriptures. Lady of Power, God has armed you with power that will allow you to remain resilient on your weight-loss journey. Keep going, knowing that everything God orchestrates will deliver His perfect will.

Sometimes, it's hard to speak words of strength, but today, Lady of Power, tell yourself, "I will only speak words of strength over my situations. I am a powerful woman designed by God to live a life of good health and well-being. I will rise above any situation that comes my way, and claim the victory before it's even over! Amen."

Your Thoughts:

_____

_____

_____

_____

_____

_____

_____

_____

_____

_____

_____

_____

_____

_____

_____

_____

_____

_____

_____

_____

_____

_____

Day *28*

It Doesn't Matter What They Say... Let Them Talk!

Have you ever experienced times when people may have said unkind words to you about an outfit, your hair, or even your size? Now, you've made a decision to change your look and work on becoming a healthier, slimmer, and even more dazzling you, but people still have something to say. Lady of Power, today you stand tall and step out there and be the powerful lady that God has called you to be! Let them talk!

Along this journey, you will meet adversity from people who try to tell you how to live your best self. There will be times that you may second guess whether you need to worry about your weight, healthier food choices, and hitting the gym. For example, you're in the fourth week of your journey. You've lost about ten pounds; you see and feel the difference, and it feels amazing! Along comes a friend – the same friend that told you that you were overweight. Instead of him or her saying you look great, they sound like this, "Girl, you don't need to lose any more weight. It's okay to have a cheat day. Your clothes look fine." They may even talk about you to other people spreading rumors of you being ill or even having surgery. But, Lady of Power, it doesn't matter what they say... let them talk!

John 10:10 says, "The thief comes only to steal and kill and destroy; I have come that they may have life, and have it to the full." (NIV) Don't let the words or even the actions of others – whether they are family, friends, co-workers, or even strangers – steal your zeal for achieving weight-loss success! This journey to a healthier you is yours and God has designed it so that He gets the glory! Often, the things people say may cause you to rethink or discourage you from continuing. Let them talk! You are too close to a permanent breakthrough to give up now. God placed this desire to live a healthier lifestyle in you for a reason. He wants you to be fit so that you can achieve success with your health goals and move on to the next assignment. You can't stop because of what others think or do! When you give in and let go of your goals by having that meal that you know is not the healthiest choice or don't share your journey with others, you're letting the enemy win. It's time to WIN by remembering that it doesn't matter what they say... let them talk!

Lady of Power, you're on a mission to live the healthiest life possible. Your ability to push past adversity in other areas of your life is now needed for your weight-loss journey. You must be determined not to let anything or anyone steal, kill, and destroy your desire to live a healthier life. The more determined you are in not letting the enemy win on your journey, the closer God will bring you to achieving the healthier life you desire. Aren't you ready to live that healthier life to the fullest? Let them talk!

Tell yourself, "I no longer rely on other people to affirm my journey. This journey is mine and I will let God guide me through. I am worthy of success!"

Your Thoughts:

Day *29*
There's POWER In Your Pain

>———>·◀———≪

Have you ever felt pain so bad that you wondered if a release would ever take place? This pain is not necessarily physical pain, but emotional pain. Emotional pain stems from broken relationships, childhood experiences, loss of a loved one, career choices, etc. This type of pain can leave one feeling broken, unwanted, depressed, hurt, angry and wondering, "Why me God?" This pain can run so deep in your mind that you want to give up fighting for what God has for you and surrender. But, Lady of Power, you must hold on! Your joy in the morning is coming. God has not forgotten you!

Lady of Power, there is POWER in your pain. Let's take a moment and reflect on Christ and what He had to endure for us to be here today, in spite of the sins we commit each day. Christ had to experience some pain by dying on the cross for our sins. In the sacrificing of His life, the whole world was able to recognize how powerful God is, because on the third day Christ rose from the dead. In His rising, all mankind received redemption. You and the entire world receive daily, the benefits of Jesus' pain. Wow! This means that no matter what you experience, no matter how painful it is, God gives you the ability to take that pain and turn it into POWER!

Romans 8:18 says, "I consider that our present sufferings are not worth comparing with the glory that will be revealed in us." (NIV) Lady of Power, you can beat anything that comes your way. No longer will you let life's challenges throw you off course. It is crucial to your weight-loss journey to meet your pain head on and lean on God for release so that your pain doesn't impede your ability to sustain a healthy lifestyle emotionally and physically. There's an old saying, "No cross, no crown!" As a woman of God, you will experience challenges; but these challenges will refine you into a woman of God that will stand with her crown as an awesome example of God's glory. Embrace the challenges that come along this journey, because they are an indication that God is still refining you and building you up to endure the assignment He has set on this earth for you. You are strong, resilient, an overcomer, and so wonderfully made that the challenges of this world can't keep you down.

Now, get up, take that pain and turn it into POWER. God wants His glory to be known through you. It's time to achieve not only your weight-loss goals but walk in the purpose God has set forth for your life! Tell yourself, "I am powerful. My pain is my POWER. I have the ability to walk this journey and be successful! Amen."

Your Thoughts:

_____

_____

_____

_____

_____

_____

_____

_____

_____

_____

_____

_____

_____

_____

_____

_____

_____

_____

_____

_____

_____

Day *30*
Take Your Journey In Bite-Sized Chunks!

Do you ever feel you're not making progress on your weight-loss journey? Do you have moments when you feel down or disappointed because you don't see immediate results? These are all valid feelings. But on this journey, you must build yourself up with a positive mindset and strategies to get you through these moments. When negative thoughts try to push their way in and make you feel like you're not making progress, you have to be able to shift your thoughts in an instant.

Lack of immediate gratification can sometimes make your weight-loss journey tough. But you have to keep in mind that immediate results may not yield a permanent lifestyle change. You must create strategies that will keep you powered up and devoted to your journey to a new you! The solution to your cravings for immediate gratification is to keep your eye on how God will grant you peace and permanent results.

One strategy that will make you feel like you're making progress is to create mini goals. Mini goals are your short-term goals that you create for yourself along the weight-loss journey. These goals will keep you encouraged, motivated, and committed to achieving success week to week! What short-term goals will you create for yourself? Lady of Power, it's time to take your journey in bite-sized chunks. In taking this action, you'll feel accomplished each week or month as you chip away at the pounds and celebrate your mini triumphs along the way.

I Corinthians 9:24 says, "Do you not know that in a race all the runners run, but only one gets the prize? Run in such a way as to get the prize." (NIV) Lady of Power, God wants the best for you! He wants you to be healthy so that you can do His work. God gives you opportunities each day – whether it is to make healthy choices or other life choices – He's looking for you to run a good race! You must push through and demonstrate your ability to WIN and FINISH well. Commit yourself wholeheartedly to your weight-loss journey, pray daily, read His word daily, and strive each day, in bite-sized chunks, towards your goals.

Tell yourself, "I am only competing against myself. I will take this journey chunk by chunk until I WIN this race. Amen."

Your Thoughts:

Day *31*
Lady Of Power, Stand In Your POWER

≫———▶·◀———≪

If you're reading this Mind, Body, & Power Inspiration, it means you've made it to Day 31! Congrats! Lady of Power, you have pushed through the month, studied God's word, prayed, and affirmed yourself. Now, you're ready to continue your journey to being the woman of God He is calling you to be! Lady of Power, stand in your POWER, with the Holy Spirit, knowing that you are capable of continuing your journey to a healthier, stronger, positive, and extra sexy you!

This book would not be complete without the Proverbs 31 scripture! Proverbs 31:25 says, "She is clothed with strength and dignity, and she laughs without fear of the future." (NLT) What a powerful scripture! Take a moment and reread this scripture. After reflecting on it, it's safe to conclude that God created you for this journey! At times, you may question why God allows certain circumstances to come into your life. You may go through several emotions and wonder if the sunshine will ever come. You may even feel like giving up because you just don't have the strength to fight. But, Lady of Power, this scripture proves that God created you with strength (which is power) and dignity (which is self-worth).

This scripture reminds us of how important it is to smile and cast all of your worries on the Lord because God has a bright future ahead of you! Stay focused on your journey to a healthy you. You, Lady of Power, stand in your POWER, with faith in what God has in store for your future. Rejoice because He is the Lord and your life is going to be awesome!

Remember, you must fight, persevere, and be determined to meet your weight-loss goals. You have to be fit for your journey. So, if you need continued inspirations and motivations, go back and start with Day 1 or choose to read them in whatever order the Spirit moves you to read them. This journey is yours. Embrace it, laugh, and let your journey be an inspiration to someone else! You can do this. YOU HAVE THE POWER.

Now look in the mirror and boldly stand and say, "I am a woman of strength and dignity, and I am excited and faithful about what God has in store for my future! I will stand in my POWER and be the Lady of Power that God has designed me to be. Transformation is mine! Amen."

Your Thoughts:

Lady Of Power Scripture List

Day

1. Philippians 4:13

2. James 2:24

3. Proverbs 3:6

4. Ephesians 2:10/Jeremiah 1:5

5. Romans 8:28

6. Jeremiah 29:11

7. Isaiah 41:10

8. Joshua 1:9

9. Mark 11:23

10. 1 Corinthians 6:19

11. Proverbs 4:25

12. Habakkuk 2:2

13. Hebrews 11:1

14. Proverbs 21:5

15. Ephesians 3:20-21

16. Genesis 2:2

17. Matthew 19:26

18. Hebrews 10:35

19. Psalm 100:3

20.   1 Peter 5:8

21.   Psalm 73:26

22.   Hebrews 10:36

23.   1 Thessalonians 5:16-18

24.   2 Corinthians 5:17

25.   1 Corinthians 10:13

26.   Romans 12:2

27.   Psalm 18:32

28.   John 10:10

29.   Romans 8:18

30.   1 Corinthians 9:24

31.   Proverbs 31:25

Your Thoughts:

About The Author

Tiffany Kelly is a multifaceted millennial woman with a career ranging from educating impressionable minds in New York City Public Schools to instructional coaching for teachers in the Atlanta Public School system. She holds a Master of Education in Mathematics from Cambridge College in addition to her Business Management degree from St. John's University. Tiffany's numerous honors and awards are a testament to the work that she has done in her more than thirteen years dedicated to improving education in schools and ensuring students' success by conducting student workshops, facilitating technology integration, and performing critical district training.

Striving for excellence in her personal life, Tiffany set out on a mission to lead a healthier lifestyle and eliminate health issues caused by weight. Her steadfast faith in God and Christian walk played a significant role in her own dynamic journey to losing more than eighty pounds. The high blood pressure medications that she had been on for nearly twelve years are a thing of the past. Tiffany believes that nothing is by accident, everything is for God's divine purpose to be manifested in each of our lives. An eagerness to share her experiences with faith and fitness led Tiffany to group fitness training as well as working with women who desire to live a healthier lifestyle. She taught fitness classes for women under one of Atlanta's top personal trainers for more than two years. She quickly became the go-to coach for providing tips, strategies, and resources to help women on their weight-loss journey.

With a unique skill-set that is unparalleled, Tiffany is dubbed the Mind, Body & Power Coach. As a result of her inspirational journey and desire to help women believe in their ability to live healthier lives by losing weight while staying empowered by the word of God, Tiffany founded Loose the Power Within! It is a one-on-one coaching service that incorporates spirituality in helping women break through barriers and live a healthy life without limits. Tiffany's constant desire to study God's word and share His word with the world helps her to have a greater impact when working with her clients.

Tiffany is a powerful speaker, a seasoned teacher, an educational leader, and a charismatic life change agent. She inspires audiences by sharing how changing her mindset and putting God first was key in changing her relationship with food and fitness. When speaking to captivated crowds, she shares tips for breaking barriers, eating to stay fit, and personal determination. Tiffany illustrates how the impact of spiritual empowerment together with a changed mindset can equal weight-loss achievement and lifelong success.

When she is not helping to shape the best life for clients, Tiffany can be found pursuing other entrepreneurial endeavors via her custom weave and wig company, *Hair Fancies*, creating healthy recipes to try out or indulging in vintage shopping. She also finds great pleasure and balance from spending time with family and friends.

Coming Soon!

- The Lady of Power Weight-loss Success Meetup Group

- Mind, Body & Power Coaching Courses for Weight-loss Transformation

- A Cookbook of Healthy Recipes for Weight-loss Success (Title Coming Soon!)

Stay connected by visiting…

Websites:
www.loosethepowerwithin.com

www.ladyofpower.com

Facebook:
https://www.facebook.com/loosethepowerwithin

Instagram:
@TiffanyKelly_LPW

Twitter:
@TKellyLPW